Masterpieces In Progress

by
Yasmine Alfred
Copyright © 2015 Yasmine Alfred

All Paintings, Drawings and Images by
Yasmine Alfred

All rights reserved.

ISBN-13: 978-0692477434

ISBN-10: 0692477438

Cover design, book design and layout By Yasmine Alfred
Edited By Allie Carico

Dedication

To my 8 year old daughter Angelina, who is a book worm. She encouraged me in the process and is very excited about this book.

Angelina,

May you always be blessed, may you always be favored, and may you always be faithful.
May you stay forever young.

May you always be silly and childish though have that adult-like soul.

May you always be humane, may you always be kind, and may you always shine for Jesus. May you stay forever my young, my baby girl! Love others just like you would love yourself.
May you stay forever young.

May you always strive to be perfect through your Heavenly Father. May you know though that life is not. May you stay forever young.

May I always be an abiding mom, may I always be a friend, may I always know you are a favor and not a possession. May I raise you to be who you are, not who I want you to be.
May I, too, stay forever young.

Introduction

In this book I will talk about you and me—us. It's not my personal story; it's ours. For I am like you: I would like to be a human before being a woman. You will find me shift from I to you a lot. It's not a mistake, or a typo, or a defect in my composition. I was blessed to be trusted from people I know that shared a lot of stories and emotions with me, and I have realized we all struggle the same but differently. This book is about us trying to reprehend our differences and share our struggles.

I first put it in art; then I elaborated with words. Words versus art—which is stronger? They say a picture is worth a thousand words, and I agree, but I say too, an apt word can be made into a thousand pictures.

I hope you enjoy reading and glancing through this book.I have enjoyed making it for you...for us.

Yasmine Alfred

I have typically viewed editing as an opportunity to help others grow. I generally feel fulfilled in helping others perfect their craft and look forward to the opportunity to teach in the process. This time, however, was quite different. During the course of editing Yasmine's book, I realized that I was the one given an opportunity to grow. Her words and art impacted me in a way I have never experienced before throughout the editing process. I often found myself rereading portions not simply to edit but to soak in the truth and preciousness of her heart's expression. I consider myself blessed to have been a part of this important, impactful, and intentional creation, and I will forever be affected in a positive way because of it. I pray you are too!

Allison Carico
Editor

CONTENTS

	Page
Masterpiece	10
Work In Progress	12
Love	14
The Art Of Love	16
Love Me A lot	18
My Enemy	20
Do You Like Me	22
Awake My Soul	23
Imprisoned	24
Seen	26
Seek No Crown	28
Fool's Paradise	30
Missing Piece	32
Silve Tears	34
Content	36
My Heart is Heavy	38
The wounded Self	40
Forgiveness	42
Letting Go	44
Empathy	46
Sometime	48
Still	51
A Lover Of Life	52
Earth	54
Complete Me	56
Hole To Whole	59
Not Yours	61
Rich & Needy	63
Paradoxical	65

Yasmine Alfred

You & Me	**67**
Eyes Of Mercy	**69**
Family	**71**
Knots	**73**
Scared & Sacred	**75**
A Story	**77**
Feeling Stuck	**79**
Excerise	**81**
Mindfulness	**83**
Transformation	**85**
A Dream	**87**
Upside Down	**89**
My Name	**91**
Volcano	**93**
Hope	**95**
Addiction	**97**
Free	**99**
Surrender	**101**
Rise & Shine	**103**
Beauty From Ashes	**105**
The Perfect Place	**107**

Masterpieces In Progress

Masterpiece

You are uniquely made. You are not a mass production. I am personally hand crafted. When He was done carving me, He broke the mold. He did the same with you. You too are loved; you are precious.

You can't be anyone else. You are a masterpiece the way you are, yet he is not done with you. You are a work in progress.

We will meet failure—feel incomplete at times. Even when you feel unheard, unseen, worthless and with no purpose, STILL you are a magnum opus to Him.

"For we are God's masterpiece. He has created us anew in Christ Jesus, so we can do the good things he planned for us long ago." Ephesians 2:10

Speaking as an artist, I am never satisfied with my piece of art. I always feel it's not finished. I want to change this, add that, reach perfection, yet never did I receive that feeling of satisfaction. However, I feel as though I own it beyond as a mere possession. It's my child; it's part of me. Even if I sold it, still it's mine. It's a piece of my time, my effort, my feelings. I want people to treat it right, appreciate it and know its worth. God feels the same way towards us but not with self-righteousness like I expressed. His sense of ownership is more out of wanting the best for you. He wants you to enjoy His creation.

"Next time a sunrise steals your breath or a meadow of flowers leave you speechless, remain that way. Say nothing, and listen as Heaven whispers, 'Do you like it? I did it just for you.'"— Max Lucida

I too am made for you—a masterpiece to give, serve, and enjoy.

A Work in Progress

Who am I in the eyes of others? Give me your eyes to see me the way you do. Who am I in my own head? Unfinished. I am a work in progress.

Have you ever asked yourself this question: Who am I in the eyes of others? It's good to listen to those who love you and who are trustworthy. There is room for change. We are all a work in progress. Even if you are 99 years old, you are still a work in progress. Forget what's behind and look ahead.

Is it even possible for one to reach perfection? Not at all, because the moment you feel you are perfect, then you need to work on humility. I will always think of myself as a very precious piece of art that continually strives for more. Our Grand Master Artist has work yet to do in and through me. Although I am His masterpiece, I am not yet complete.

We might be a brilliant painting, but perhaps we choose to hide in the garage, left to dust. I will share my beauty; I will choose to love and hang around with other paintings that balance me out and cause me to shine.

Love

Whether or not you believe God exists is not what I am here to convince you of. I am not a preacher or even close to perfect.

But first consider this. Personally, I feel the immense love inside me cannot be just a coincident. This massive, limitless beauty and love can't be there without a creator. This joy of life and being can't just be there. Someone greater shall be the master of this precious heart of mine—to teach, to tame, and to process how to guard it and share it. And that's the belief of my heart—my precious, beautifully made heart. This satisfies my soul.

Love is not what we have been told from others who have been hurt or do not know Love. We blame Love. Love is not just an emotion; Love is joy. Love is strength. Love is very kind. Love is forgiving and very patient. Love is not just a solution. Love is Life.

Arabic Calligraphy on the Painting:

1 Corinthians 13:4-8

Love is patient, love is kind. It does not envy, it does not boast, it is not proud. It does not dishonor others, it is not self-seeking, it is not easily angered, it keeps no record of wrongs. Love does not delight in evil but rejoices with the truth. It always protects, always trusts, always hopes, always perseveres. Love never fails.

تتأنى وتزرق
تجسد
تقنع
ستقنع
تقنع
تختنق
تطلب ما لنفسك
تغرق بالحق
سوى
ثانية
كل شيء
يحتمل
تصدق
تصبر على

The Art of Love

Vincent van Gogh said, "There is nothing more artistic than to love people."

Connect, pray, carry, shield, serve, and enjoy each other. Share your love. We need each other in community. You need me; I need you. You cannot fulfill your purpose for yourself without others. I need others to walk with, to serve, and to serve with. We were never meant to walk in life alone.

I am not talking about being married or single. There are a lot of married people who feel lonely and a lot of singles who do not.

Take pleasure in others, delight in others' success, learn from them. Make your words words of encouragement, words of praise. Choose gentleness even though, not because.

Use your hands to lift, and if you ever scream, scream to seek and praise. Don't demand from others; demand from yourself to live in harmony, but first live in harmony with yourself.

We fail everyday to accept others. Create your own boundaries, not by saying NO but by choosing what to listen to—filter: thus blocking the negative so that you may thrive. Know your limits, your worth, and the rules to identify what's safe for you and how to react peacefully yet firmly when someone steps on your limits. Live to the fullest, live in harmony, and dance with life.

Love Me a Lot

Careful! Do not misunderstand—I am not seeking to be loved from another. I will love me a lot.

You are who you are: loud or quite, social or introverted, a noble prize winner or 7th grader. Like me or not, I can't be anyone or anything but what I was created to be.

We were taught that whoever loves himself is proud and is lacking humility. To quote C.S. Lewis, "Humility is not thinking less of yourself, it is thinking of yourself less."

You are uniquely created, wonderfully and fearfully made. Love the creator in you.

I have learned I will never be able to love anyone even if he/she is perfect (which is impossible) unless I make friends with myself—unless I know me, fathom my soul, am kind to myself, have hunger to make myself better everyday with every breath.

"Love your neighbor as yourself." God didn't ask you to love others and abandon yourself. Love yourself through Him, so that you would be able to love your neighbor fully and righteously. Unless I love me, I won't be ably to love you. Unless I make friends and am at peace with me, I will not be able to do the same with you.

I will love me a lot, aim not to please anyone but the One who made me. I will not make my focus on applause or criticism but rather upon wanting to be a masterpiece for the Artist who created me.

My Enemy

If you would define the word enemy, you would likely come up with a definition like "a person who is actively opposed to or hostile toward someone or something." What's one of our worst enemies? It's when our own spirit serves as our own prosecutor and attacker.

This inner enemy comes across as those inside voices yelling, trampling every single hope of grace and goodness inside us telling us lies like; you are not good enough, smart enough, or beautiful enough. You are not alone. It happens to most of us, but what makes you a conqueror is talking back to your enemy and refuting the lies that are being spoken over you.

What if I am not perfect? Well, no one is. Learn to recognize the signs of your own fear and failure. Make a decision and change what is causing you to destroy your confidence instead of abiding with it. It's not an outside enemy. It is the enemy within if you believe the lies. You have the power to thwart that enemy.

Do You Like Me?

I am who I am: I will be genuine, I speak the truth, I will not try to be someone I am not or feel something I don't. I will scream, I will cry, I will laugh deeply from the heart. I am a human, I am a woman, I am not an object, but watch out. I still might break. I will not care what you think of me because I have enough guilt boiling inside of me.

I am a masterpiece, like me or not.

Awake, My Soul

Awake, your soul! Live in the present—in the NOW. Know that thinking won't change the present obstacle. On the other hand, if it ever changes anything, it will execute your exciting moment.

Over-thinking, worrying, and being anxious are mankind's best friends. They make you unable to enjoy the present moment. This means you are half dead. It feels like you are accomplishing things, running errands, seeing friends; but your mind is so drowned, trying to swim and survive in the ocean of dwellings. The SHOULD HAVE, COULD HAVE, WOULD HAVE will kill you.

Resurrect, give birth to a dream, and renew the breath of life. Have an awakened soul.

Imprisoned

When the poison of life blinds you and the sin sinks in to your bones, you won't be able to see beauty. You won't be able to hear love. You will only see things in your crooked way. "Cold and bitter is the world," you will say.

All you will see is darkness, negativity, and ugliness. I can't handle the past; I can't see the future. These negative thoughts will pervade your mind. Everything will pull you down. The only music you will hear and dance to will be with the devil's. He will rob you of your sight, and he will deafen your ears.

Where did my sight go? Where is the sun that used to shine so brightly? I am afraid to be manipulated. I am afraid to be hurt, I am afraid to be misunderstood, afraid to be abused. I am afraid of the truth that is imprisoned in my soul, scared that anyone would see it. I am afraid of myself and my ability to damage all that's good. So I will shut down, and when you talk, I will block it out. *LALALALALALA!*

It's interesting how we as humans respond. When we are afraid, we guard ourselves with self-harming tricks. It's like we are so used to misery and pain that we want to recreate it over and over because that's what we are used to. We get so comfortable being uncomfortable that we relive your painful past and recreate it for yourself again. Being a victim makes us feel our self-worth. And then we whine, hiss, and make your own agonized prophecy.

If you want people to change, you change. Take off your darkened glasses; see your lover's eyes—see a beautiful future ahead. Remove that plug in your ear. Listen to the music of love others are trying to sing to you. For your comfort zone is manipulating you and blocking out all who love you.

Make a promise to yourself—promise to give your future a chance. Revive, renew, and resurrect your soul to relive in peace again.

Seen

Needing to be seen and working to attain this need with persistence and great demand is like a little child who nags, begs, and pounds for attention.

The moment you stop feeling incomplete and abandoning your inner self, you will discover the wonders of who you are spiritually and observe your marrow.

I won't care to be seen by others. My focus will be on how to grow, to make a better me, helping us become better for others, not to please them, but to serve them and serve the greater purpose.

It's not about indulging and satisfying myself; not at all! It's going beyond, gracefully living knowing your worth, beauty, talents, and purpose and loving to serve others, thriving to be more every day.

Seek no Crown

And when you are doing well, seek no crown.

I shall not run after my glory, people's likes, nor admiration. Don't get me wrong; I am nowhere close to perfect in this aspect, still wanting people to like me. I feel so happy, so excited, so humbled when friends like my art or speak positive and encouraging words when I do well, yet one needs to learn not to run after it—not to do something only for praise.

Let's choose good for its goodness and right for its strength, kindness for its humanity, and forgiveness for its peace. Let's make art for its beauty and writing for healing.

Fool's Paradise

Sometimes I find myself running after a lie and chasing my own bogus paradise while all I need is my own sanity and peace.

What do you mean? How come? I had to run to feed my family, to do my assignments in school, to do what I am supposed to do in life. I have to! I have responsibilities, duties, missions to run after! I understand; I do too. However, you must know your priorities, be trained to pick up what is real and what is not, be able to identify if it is a delusion or not and know what your real purpose is. For when you run, you end up chasing yourself; you will become like a dog chasing his own tail, trying faster and faster thinking the outcome will be different—as if you will be able to attain or accomplish your goal, but bogus it is.

Be your own best friend instead of chasing yourself. What? Me? My own best friend? Isn't this being full of myself rather than humble? Remember; love the creator in you. Just stop chasing the wrong target thinking you are not enough. Chasing a career is a good goal, but making a difference around your colleagues is a higher and more noble purpose. Earning an A+ on your test is such a great goal, but to help another succeed and give hope to those who struggle is a higher purpose.

I will have a purpose rather than a goal, dream, or even fantasy. I will search for the reason for which I was created because I wasn't born simply to exist. My purpose is not just to run in circles and fulfill some immediate desires. I will build my castle on Thee Rock.

Missing Piece

At times you feel like a puzzle with a missing piece—feeling incomplete, searching for the missing piece to feel complete.

People will talk in a language that you don't understand. You try to, but still you feel misunderstood.

Huh? What? I don't get it! Can anyone hear me? Can anyone see me or understand me? I didn't mean it that way. Who am I? Why do I feel like an alien, invisible. Hello! I am here! Do you understand me now? Do I even make sense now? Probably not.

You don't need to be heard. It's not like you will die if you aren't heard or seen. It's a want, not a need. First know that; then put it in perspective. When we feel this way, it's mostly because we don't really know what we want or how to say it. Start first by understanding yourself: see yourself, and seek to understand others as well.

Silver Tears

Be a human even if no one else is. Being an artist (though a lot of times I doubt I am) I feel more—I ache more. When you go through rough times, it is hard and it feels like you are alone, struggling with yourself, fighting with life.

Guilt will sometimes knock you down. You begin to believe the lie: "I cannot deal with it." People can hurt you even if they don't mean to. So you decided to treat everyone as rough as they do. Not only will you stop liking some; you will end up hating yourself.

Never treat people as they deserve because your heart does not deserve to hate. Your mind will not be able to handle the struggle anymore.

I am a mess—perfectly imperfect. The funny thing is we all are, but we like to paint ourselves in our minds as a perfect version.

For by grace I was saved, so by grace I will try to love as much as I was created to love. Your tears are heard like hollers and are high priced. They are not wasted nor ignored. They will be molded to a perfect, flawless, sterling prize.

I am not forgotten nor forsaken. I am precious.

Content

Words written on the neck—I am who I am for a reason. I am just what He wants me to be. Those things that happened in my life were there for a purpose. So I won't fear tomorrow. I will enjoy and build deep relationships. I will spend my money, use my talents, value my relationships. I am here for a little while, so I will use what was given to me. Whenever I have an opportunity, I will do good. I will encourage, support, forgive others. I will speak the truth in love, admit my mistakes, and respect others' differences.

I am who I am. A mature woman, I am—one who is known for her understanding. I will not use harmful words but only positive one. The more pleasant my words are, the more influential I shall be. I am who I am; I am here for a reason!

But what if I am not? What if I fail to follow through! We make mistakes, and for that I will forgive myself and try again. Forgiveness cannot be given unless it is obtained. Forgiveness will heal me. So I make a promise to myself to forgive myself for thinking too much or too little of myself, for forgetting to forgive others, for neglecting to forgive myself. To be content, I will forgive the times I was way too harsh or too reluctant to forgive myself. I will forgive myself for not doing all that I preach and teach. Only then will I experience contentment.

My Heart is Heavy

Walking with my heart on my sleeves, I am shackled in the middle of the world's heaviness.

I could be happy. I could be free, but what is happiness if you are happy in the middle of unhappy people.

Mend that heart that has been crushed by evil, that heart that is worn out, that heart that can't live without this smile.

Believe it or not, I am a very positive and happy person, full of life. (On a side note, I'm very funny.) But I wonder how one can be happy if constantly surrounded by wounded, unhappy people.

How can a rose flourish and shine in a bush where there are many weeds? How can one breathe if he is drowning without boundaries and has no capacity or energy for himself because he's all worn out with the world?

Take your space to listen to your soul: meditate. You will be easily shackled with any and every sound in the world otherwise.

If you are in a loud pub, you will never be able to hear your friends' whispers, just like if you live, abide, and distress in the world's dilemmas, you won't hear God's soft whispers of hope and growth.

Devote a promise to yourself—to love yourself and be soft to your heart by giving yourself the space to enjoy your being and quiet your soul from the shackles of life.

The Wounded Self

The wounded will wound back causing one to wonder who started first.

When you get hurt, sometimes to cope, you may do tricks that you are unaware of—projecting your feelings on others, shutting down from your emotions, shutting others down so you won't be hurt ever again. You may find yourself acting cold and lifeless, or you may make everyone responsible for your own unsatisfied soul, worry, and unhappy.

Your wounded self can hurt you. You might be aggressive, trying to devour all who come near you, or perhaps you become very defensive—anytime, anywhere, even when it's not really needed.

Your wounded self can hurt you; you may be a victim of your own self. Then you would want to hurt people back so they can taste a piece of your misery or you may even hurt them not meaning to, just because you yourself are sore.

It's like saying, "I am all good. I have no problem; it's all them." All the while, you are wearing a crown of thorns proudly yet painfully thinking you are a victim and everyone is there to get you.

Remove that soreness— your thorn, that sharp blade inside your soul—and you will survive your own agony. Hoers won't get to you. Heal and sigh no more.

Forgiveness

I can see your inequities. Your sin is all I see now, but I still want to forgive you.

Forgiveness is not minimizing the hurt, for this is a cheap imitation. It's not when someone says, "I am sorry. Please forgive me," because this is wanting something in return, to be able to forgive. It means to "For Give,"—to give ahead. To forgive is not to forget the hurt; only God forgets. We are merely humans; we tend not to forget.

Forgiveness is not trusting instantly. Forgiveness is a decision. The act of forgiveness, however, does not take time. On the other hand, trust can take a lot of time to be rebuilt. You can forgive and let go for your own health and well-being. Forgiveness is needed for your own sanity and your own heart. Remember, forgiveness is not wanting to get even.

…but leave room for God's wrath.

Let's say someone gave you a bomb. Instead of throwing it far far away, you take it and tuck it in your heart or throw it back at them. What will happen? You will either end up exploding your own self, and the offender will run for his life, or you will end up bombing the offender, and you won't be a victim anymore. You will be the attacker and the aggressor. Not forgiving makes you miserable and bitter, and if you don't let go, you will end up being like the one who hurt you. You will not only hate them; you will end up hating yourself as well.

It's so hard. I know—very! What can make forgiveness harder?

Expectations. Expectations make forgiveness harder. When the pain comes from the closest, forgiveness is harder. When attacks come from those you love and those you think the best of, forgiveness is harder and harder. With the repetition of wrong over and over, forgiveness becomes hardest. When the attacker doesn't feel sorry, forgiveness seems impossible, and the weight can feel almost unbearable.

When you don't forgive, you will worry. You will get sick. You will be anxious. You might even get depressed. It's hard to forgive, but it's dangerous not to. You can't forgive unless you stick to Christ, melt with God, become one with Him, depend on Him, and see through His eyes. When you choose forgiveness, you choose God, and ultimately, you choose life.

Letting Go

Let go, and let God. How can I do this? Let Him lead. Think less of the hurt; focus more on God's great plans for you to change. Surrender, and be meek.

How come? Just pages ago I said love yourself; be kind to yourself. Am I contradicting myself? Not at all.

Meekness is not weakness. To be meek means you have all the strength and power under God's control. Meekness is loving yourself so much that you choose not to hurt yourself rather than holding tightly to your pain and chaining yourself to more misery. On the other hand, weakness is having no strength at all.

How can I have the strength to let go then?

We can't go back in time and change history, so letting go would be easier. We cannot change the past, for the past is in the past. We cannot receive what we can't give. It's only the love of God that can allow you to let go. Refill your heart with His love so that you will be able to let go. Keep on giving forgiveness; repeat it over and over—seventy times seven times until the pain fades away and completely vanishes. Love your heart and forgive. Let go of all the chains and burdens.

Focus on God, and your freedom, wellness, and joy. Letting go will be much easier then. It will be natural, not forced nor feared.

I haven't found my wellness and real joy until I let go of all my hurts and hang ups.

Empathy

Empathy is the ability to understand and share the feelings of another. It is a curse that I wouldn't want to give up.

For a long time I thought that it was normal to have empathy for others. It was just what everyone was supposed to do. I feel her; his vibes affect me; their pain pains me. Then you get lost in the middle of those troubles. I will practice to use it wisely, learn more to guard myself and walk away from insensitive people. For one can only control his behaviors, not others. Set boundaries. Feel for others, but don't carry them home with you. Try not to allow feeling for others affect you negatively. One won't help if he is weak. In strength we can aide. By breaking we won't mend.

I won't serve anyone by worrying about everyone, by carrying the burden of their pain on my shoulders. Fell their pain, give them love, or give them an ear, but keep your soul from the excess baggage. I promise I will feel, but I will save my heart from the grievance of the odds and ends of pain.

Lastly, before I say anything more, I will put myself in others' shoes and see if what I say or do could hurt someone or not. I've made the mistake of forgetting to do so a lot. It's ok. Try again. Listen, listen, and listen again. Don't give advice unless you are asked to. Filter, pray, and—one more time—listen,.

Sometimes

Sometimes I feel crippled, anxious, unworthy, and unable; other times I feel forgiven and alive—as though I can fly and conquer the world. I can get lost in the ocean of my emotions.

Sometimes all that controls me is emotion, but I was given a mind too, so I need to use both with balance. Satan will take advantage of you; his happiest moments are when he has control over your feelings, and he makes you believe the lies you tell yourself; bitterness, worry, failure, hate, shame, and guilt all pervade your mind and soul. If you give in, you will allow your feelings to dominate you; they will become your god.

I have an enormous amount of emotions. I don't have to believe all that I feel. I can't make my emotions and feelings lead me; however, I can allow my emotions to manipulate me if I'm not careful. If I have no manager over my feelings, I will be a mess.

Imagine yourself as a business. If you don't have a manager or a boss to lead you or someone to hold you accountable, the business will fail. Even if you own your own business, if you don't manage it, your business will still fail: a country without a leader, a house without walls.

How can I deal then with how I feel? This is a good question to ask yourself. It's a skill we need to get the knack of: managing our unleashed feelings.

I teach my kids that they have the right to feel anything and everything, even anger and jealousy. I validate their feelings first; then we identify the root, but we just can't not act upon it. Rather we challenge ourselves to change the situation. No shame in how you feel, but deal with it positively.

First we have to know what the feeling is because how can I mange something without knowing what it is?! As the common expression goes, "If you can't name it, you can't tame it." What's the real reason for it? Then ask yourself, "Why do I feel this? What triggered it? Is this feeling true or false?" If you can't talk to yourself about it, it will control you and the people around you. You may even end up dumping it on your relationships and the people around you. You will accuse others for your emotions and how you feel. Will that feeling help me grow or is it self-defeating, a self-fulling prophecy to destroy myself? If you want to succeed, you can't keep telling yourself that you are a failure. Challenge yourself to change those distracting and harmful feelings. Take accountability of each feeling you have: name the lies you tell yourself, make boundaries for the lies that you have been told. Then you will not find yourself swaying any longer with those emotion.

It is I who has those unclear, untamed feelings. It is I who will tame it through God's help. I will choose to use all of my feelings for the good of myself and others.

Still

In Your hands I am carried; in Your palm I am safe.

"For I am the Lord your God who takes hold of your right hand and says to you, 'Do not fear; I will help you.'" Isaiah 41:13

We sometimes put our troubles and problems in man's arms—being dependent and not able to deal with our own feelings, thinking man's love is enough. Well, he loves me, I have nothing to worry about, and if troubles hit, together we can fix it, right? Wrong. I have learned that some situations and hopes are nightmares masked as daydreams. If you depend on man, you will stumble because we all fall: we are all weak by ourselves; we are all imperfect in ourselves.

The only constant and non changeable is my Creator. He knows my wounds, my imperfection, my pain, and your pain that was caused by other wounded humans. He is the only one that offers unconditional love. He will carry us in His arms. Invest your love in Him, for where you invest your love, you invest your soul.

A Lover of Life

I will teach her how to love life and enjoy it and love the Creator and praise Him.

You may be told that to love God is to be not of the world. I agree but if I may put it in a different perspective for you, to love God is to love earth and each corner of it—to enjoy its beauty, celebrate life by loving its beauty, to praise with each breath of fresh air.

It's true that I will live in the world, but I won't make the world live in me. It's that thin line that makes a great difference.

I will teach my daughter to love, to appreciate, to dance and jump with joy. I will teach her to see the greens and blues in nature and praise and enjoy, to watch and observe every color her eyes shall meet; and her eyes shall be filled with smiles knowing it was all done for us to enjoy and to be pleased by the Maker of this art. I will teach her to love other fellow humans and enjoy them, know that we are made to be different but shall live in the harmony of love.

Loving life here does not mean one loves the material world. Yes, material serves us, and I will be grateful for it every day, but it is not the source of my joy. Look beyond. Not a lover of things in life—A Lover Of Life.

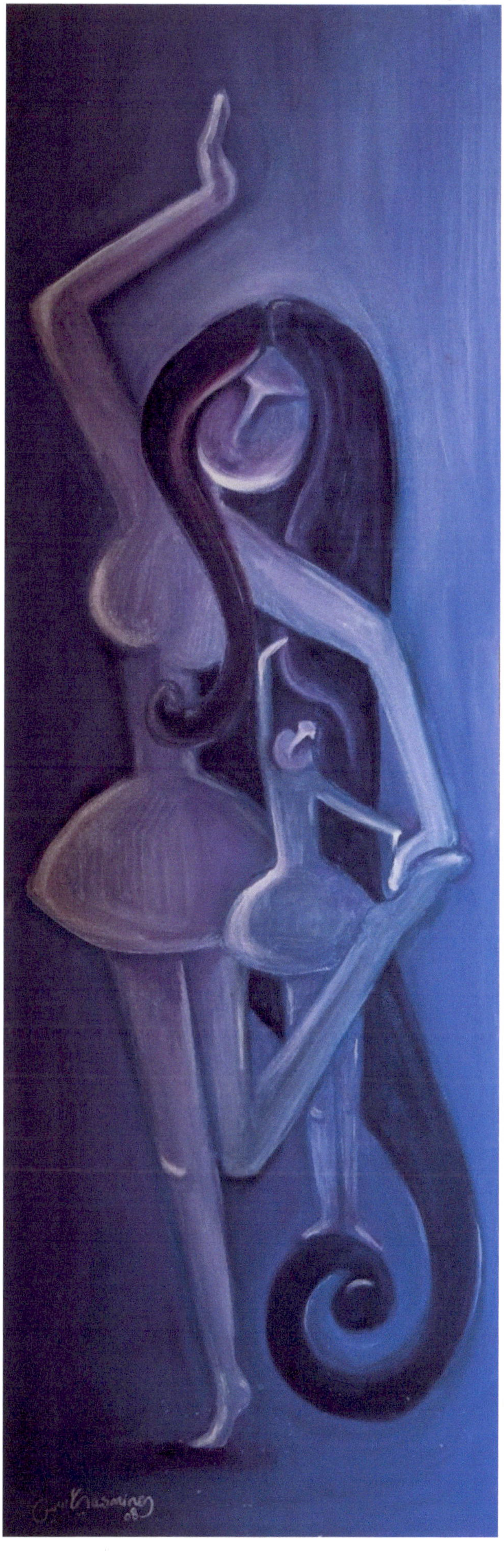

53

Earth

Earth is who we are; don't just live on earth; make earth part of who you are. You take care of your body, so it takes care of you. Earth and its living beings are the bigger picture of your body. So take good care of your earth, my earth and our earth. There is no earth that holds you down; there is no place that can contain you. We live in it, but the earth shall never live in us.

I am nature.

I am the sea.

I am the sun.

I am the mountain.

I am water; I am fire.

I might be nobody to you, but I am a star for my Maker.

I am earth, but earth can't contain me.

You don't get me; it's ok. Neither can I.

Complete Me

No one will ever complete you unless you pick your own pieces.

A hole in your soul will make a whole lot of trouble in your relationship. Your heart will never be a home if you have a gaping hole in it. That void no one will ever fill. With these types of voids, emptiness and loss of purpose, you will build an empire on air, an empire of dust that wind may blow—a castle of unhealthy love built on dependency, quiet rage, anger, frustration, shallowness, and above all neediness.

You chose a partner. Let's imagine here that this partner is a piece of perfect, delicious chocolate cake. Yummm! Then you add to it vinegar and continue to munch on it only to find out it is sour and horrible. You blame the cake, forgetting you poured the vinegar here. You are the vinegar: the sour, the bitter. Unless you focus on your mistake and resolve to fix it, you won't enjoy a yummy partner.

Let's use our imaginations again here. It's like putting a lot of water on the roots of a plant that has been dead for weeks, hoping it will flourish again, or putting spices on a rotten piece of chicken hoping it will become edible that way, or putting two pieces of torn and holed papers from the same place on top of each other hoping one will cover the other's hole. Start from scratch, a complete new healed soul, instead of trying to redo, rewind, and mix healthy with unhealthy. Grow a new seed, a new plant, a whole new blank paper. Save your savory spices for a fresh piece of meat instead of waisting your energy and weeping more over a bad meal. Add the right ingredient to your yummy cake instead of sobbing over the ruined remains. Restart, renew, and restore. And Enjoy.

Don't pour all of your energy in the wrong direction trying to fix someone else while you need to be complete first.

The void can get bigger if we focus on the other's inability to fill our void until it becomes unbearable to live together. Don't compensate; evaluate and reshape.

Get it! Be liberated, freed from fixing another! We can't defeat insecurities overnight. It takes time, dedication, and hard work, but the outcome is so rewarding. I promise. Pick yourself up, fill your void, rebuild yourself, face your imperfection, remold yourself in a whole manner. Embrace the hardship of your remaking. Bloom. Fill your void first; help yourself so you would be able to deal with the imperfections of others.

Hole to Whole

We all have a hole in our hearts. If we try to fix it through the means of the world or by the help of others, this may rust it and dirty it more.

Hmmm...let me see what I can fill this hole with? I can fill it with a big crowd and laughter; maybe it will disappear that way. Or maybe I can fill it with a relationship. Or perhaps I can fill it with lies, ignoring that the hole even exists. But how can we love when we are scared? Oh, I've got it! Let's run in circles keeping ourselves busy with work, money, friends, social life, etc. Surely that will fill me up!

Well, nothing worked. It was like a momentary satisfaction. Then when we are alone again, we weep over our fear, emptiness, and how life has left us unfulfilled and unsatisfied.

So how can I fix this? How can I fill the hole?

God heals. He can make all things new and wash away the past. How can I fill the hole? The simple answer is that I can't. Only He can. In Him I am complete. I am an incomplete piece, a masterpiece in progress, but in Him the hole will be made whole, and I will be healed.

Not Yours

I am not an object. I am more than a sweet melody you play for enjoyment. I am more than a pet you keep around for amusement. I am not all yours. I am a human; I am a woman. Some things seem to be more beautiful than they really are: they deceive you and leave you crippled—a perfect figure for someone else but not for yourself.

At times you feel so protected—you are loved yet sheltered and perhaps even smothered. Sheltering might cause you to cave in to being someone you are not. Don't blame those who treat you like they own you or those who play you. You have a will power to break though and say, "I own myself, and no one else is in control of me, my behavior, or my reactions."

Unless you are a robot, your feelings will be hurt." Abusers can't offend, brain wash, or gaslight you if you feel your true worth and treat yourself right. When you know your true value, you won't let this negativity affect you or sink into your soul. Leave and refuse to accept their insults. Instead of weeping and sticking around for more abuse, trust your intuition and your true value.

Rich and Needy

What will I win if I gain the whole world but lose myself?

Running after people to gain their approval, working hard to earn more so people will respect you more, praise you more, like you more: ever been there before?

How many of us want to be more, so much so that we find ourselves running and running to feel whole again, not knowing we are going in the wrong direction, filling this heart with junk that will leave us more hungry.

Your heart screams, "LOVE ME! ACCEPT ME! LET ME FIT IN!" You work so hard; you beg for anyone and everyone's attention, yet your head says, "I don't care. I have everything I need. I am better than them. Why should I care?"

That's when the core problem happens: your heart is not aligned with your thoughts. What you want rationally seems wrong but your heart and mind tells you something contrary.

Love YOU! Accept YOU! If you fill your own void with the Father's love, you will win yourself back. For the world is full of poison that will infiltrate you with its neediness at your very roots. However, Christ is the giver of life who will inject you with His love—His freedom from the ways of this world.

Paradoxical

What will you gain if you run as fast as you can only to find out you are running in the wrong direction?

We can all think of that tangible or intangible thing that we believe will fulfill our deepest need if we can just attain it. We wait and wait in deep need for things, that our eyes gloss over what we already have—something that might be way more satisfying, healthier, and more fulfilling.

Let me tell you about my dog. He has this bowl that is full of good, nutritious food. His bowl is full, yet he leaves it for hours, getting hungrier and hungrier. He would prefer to lick my hands or the crumbs that fall from my plate. He would rather lick the dirty crumbs off the floor that are sometimes nothing more than sandy little pieces of bread. Still, he chooses to leave his chicken with rice (dog food) that is full of vitamins that will make him live longer and healthier. He only eats it when he is so overcome by hunger that he has no other option. Now let's all make fun of the dog. No, let's not. How pathetic...right?

How many of us do the same thing? We chase, run after, and want to munch on contaminated crumbs, leaving that perfect meal untouched just in front of our eyes.

The sin seems so much more appealing even though it will ultimately end up leaving us broken. We need that thing so badly that it will leave us shattered: we want, we need, we run, and ultimately we get so weary. We only start really knowing what we have when we hit rock bottom with exhaustion. By glorifying the hunger, settling for crumbs, we achieve the paradoxical effect of making us satisfied.

Aren't we funny! Or should I say, how pathetic, right? We stay focused on wanting and being exhausted from chasing. Go the right direction. Use your spiritual GPS wired within, and you will never lose out on the spiritual sustenance we have within. Recalculating: turn right in one mile.

You can live without this unhealthy attitude. You will thrive without self-distraction. You will be better off without this job that is unsuitable for you, no matter how much money it may bring. You will taste joy when you follow what you are wired to really want instead of settling for the crumbs under the table leaving you to wonder why. Choose sustenance. Be filled with the rich nutrition your Creator has cooked up for you.

You and Me

We long for intimacy, but we long to feel safe as well. We want to have a partner to help make us feel complete, but we forget that we should be complete on our own.

We fear vulnerability, we fear exposure, we fear emotional nakedness. We fear insecurity and rejection. We become sick because of the secrets we bury deep inside, longing only to show the very best version—an inaccurate version—of ourselves. Perfect love does not include fear. If you have fear, you are not in love; you are just in excitement. As an individual in a relationship, you are not to worry or be afraid of what the other thinks of you. Have confidence; focus on love—true love. Focus on accepting yourself before you focus on the other accepting you. Risk, have the power to love again, have the courage to be open—to be vulnerable. Mistakes create opportunities for learning; they teach us lessons in humility.

Maybe as a child you were given a very little space to make mistakes. Admitting your mistakes as an adult has become very hard to do, afraid you won't be accepted or loved anymore. All that you needed as a kid were acceptance and love. Not much has changed: you still need those same two things as an adult. And if it wasn't met as a child, you will seek them as an adult from your partner. Mistakes are part of our humanity; they are crucial for our spiritual growth. Choose to grow together as a result of your mistakes, not in spite of them.

A good marriage is a union of two good forgivers—two imperfect souls who are willing to see each other with eyes of mercy, equally compromising and forgiving one another in love. To love is to see the other with eyes full of mercy and compassion.

Eyes of Mercy

Let me see you through the eyes of mercy, the eyes of love.

When I am weak, my heart becomes filled with anger and self-pity. These tears cause me to be unable to see clearly. My eyes become fickle and my vision is blurred to the point that I no longer see others through the eyes of mercy.

When I look into God's eyes, the eyes of mercy fill my soul and I remember I need forgiveness myself. That's when I realize I can't refuse to receive myself what I must give to others. So I decide again to see others through the eyes of mercy.

Showing mercy brings happiness to your soul. When you display mercy, you own peace in your heart, you nourish yourself, you are kind to your soul—and that's why you will own happiness and joy.

There is not enough mercy in this world. God wants each one of us to be an agent of His mercy, an ambassador for His love.

The idea of showing mercy can cause us to feel like we are standing in a burning building:, initially, we are paralyzed with fear—so afraid to be burned yet so afraid to jump and let go. We must choose to surrender. Weakness and loss of possessions may come to mind, but when we choose to let go, we fall into the arms of Jesus. When I look into His eyes, all I see is a reflection of me. I see the eyes of love, the eyes of mercy. That's when I realize I want to see others through His eyes—the eyes of mercy. You can't receive what you are unwilling to give. You can't ask for mercy, when you fuss and cringe when you are asked to give it to others. Just try to see others through the eyes that are full of beauty, through the eyes of mercy.

Ask yourself today: who has hurt me that I can show mercy toward? And at the same time, choose to accept mercy in the process.

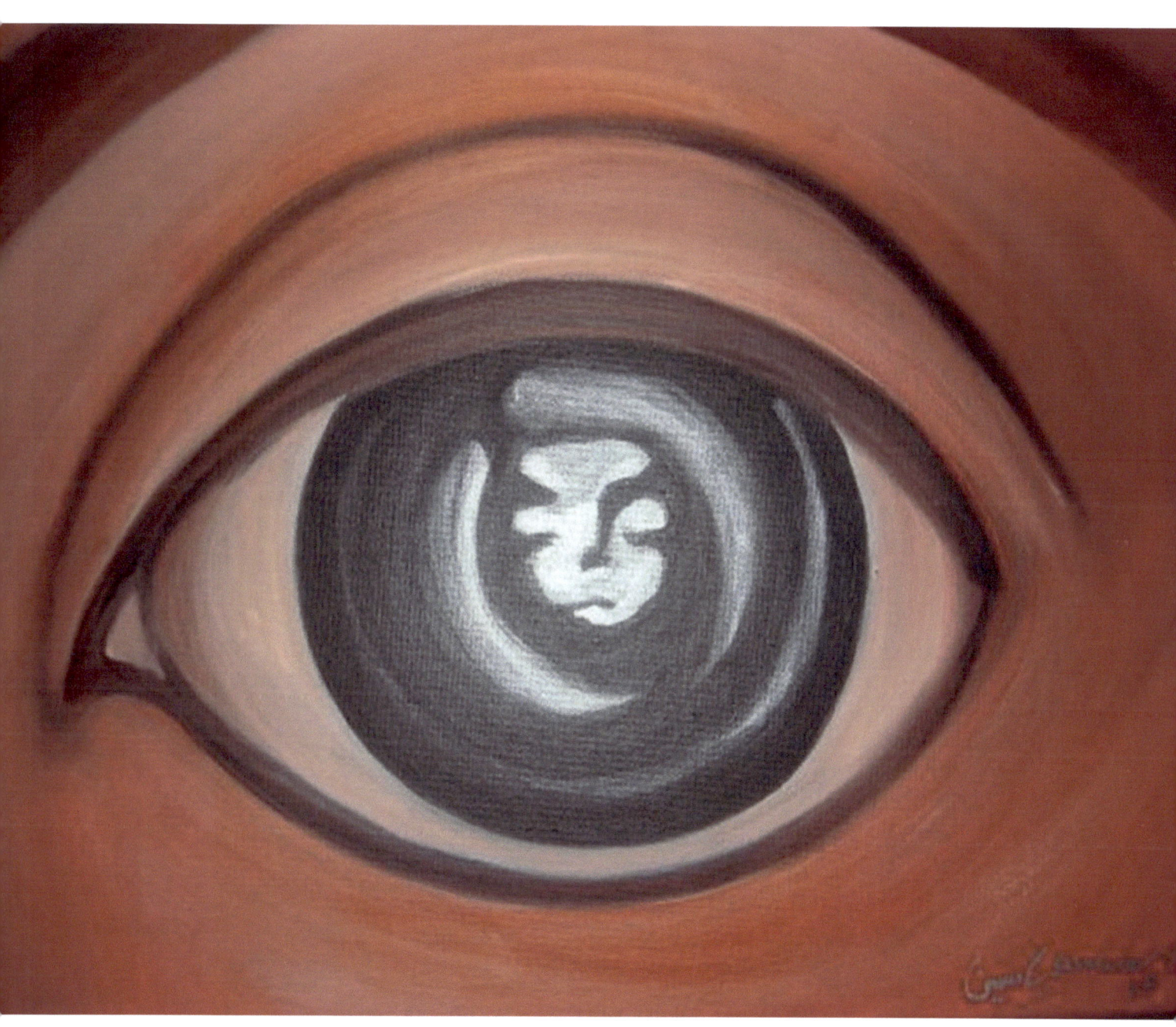

Family

A happy, balanced adult is the result of a happy childhood. A happy child is typically the byproduct of loving parents. Which comes first: the chicken or the egg?

How can we successfully become loving parents? Does it require being in a happy marriage? If that's the case, should we try to make our partner happy and as a result we become loving? What comes first: the happy child or the happy parent? Or is it about a happy self?

Let's start younger and work our way to the older. Give your children a chance to make mistakes. Correct them with love and compassion. Give them lots of hugs; you can never give too many hugs. Send them into the world with confidence and boost their self esteem, yet balance it by teaching them compassion and sympathy for others. Give your all to them, yet don't reflect to them that life is all about them only. Teach them to love themselves by loving yourself and having compassion on others as well. If they offend a friend, encourage them to ask themselves, "How do you think this made your friend feel?" Compassion makes a child merciful, respectful, and never a bully.

Let's move to the adult now. You won't be able to achieve a happy adulthood unless you were a happy child or unless the wounds of your childhood have been healed and you now love who you are. Achieving happiness as an adult generally means you have made peace with your parents if there was ill will between you and them, not wanting to relive what was done to you. Finally, to become a content couple, you have to be a healthy loving individual first.

So the chicken first or the egg? I have no idea. All I know is that a happy child typically makes a healthy, loving adult, often leading to a loving couple who brings up a happy child. And the cycle goes on.

Knots

We all have that weak point, that problem, that sin, that knot that life yields. Insecurities. Childhood wounds.

Face your imperfect soul instead of facing others' imperfection. I know I have said it before. No one will unknot you. Imagine yourself as a form of software; you are your own code reader.

Seek the maker of your soul. He can help you; He is the Healer, the Doctor and the Creator.

The moment you focus on others saying, "They did that to me, he hurt me, she scarred me, they pained me. I have all these knots that are suffocating me and making me hurt and hurt others just because of them, I am a victim," no healing will come. No moving forward will happen. Keep your eyes focused on Jesus to cure what has been broken, to comfort what's been pained. Yes, I will be healthy. I will be untangled. I will be whole. I will be healed.

Scarred and Sacred

I am scarred. I am sinful. But I am treasured. I am sacred, for I am His. At times we criticize ourselves, expecting better.

We accept from others what we think we deserve. When we settle with crumbs, it's because we think that's all we can get, or that is all we deserve, leaving ourselves more scared. We play the role of victims because it satisfies us—it becomes part of our self worth, an excuse to be redundant and stay in the self pity mood because it makes us feel better about our negativity. We forget who we really are and what we deserve. Be more! Inner scars may inspire us to change and grow. Inner scars help us to be more sympathetic to others instead of wanting to be stuck in our own pain. The scar will always be there even if we've healed, but it can help us minister to those with unhealed scars that are still oozing. Only the scarred can truly feel the scarred, but only the healed will help you.

Making a choice of using your scars to help is a blessing; you change from a victim, from shame, from self pity to a compassionate human being who wants all to be sacred, safe, and sound.

I will make my scar a place to understand others. Be an overcomer instead of over whelmed.

A Story

Everybody has a story to share and a wound that needs healing.

Behind all those perfect faces and perfect lives, behind those closed doors, there are a lot of other stories. See that big smile? Behind it is a big wound that no one knows about it. No one likes to look imperfect in front of the world. Very few of us have gained enough confidence to share our stories that would help others. You may never learn about that man who was raped as a child, that woman who was cheated on, that couple that had financial issues nearly leaving them homeless—the woman also dealing with emotional abuse for years as well as physical abuse but for a great career so she feels she has to cover it up. An alcoholic husband, a mentally ill family member, divorce, or a couple living under the same roof hating each other thinking they are doing the best for the sake of their kids, a son who caused a lot of ache to his family, terminal illness, miscarriages, infertility, a child who died too soon—the list goes on. Shame and more shame. Cave in. Don't show emotion. Act as if everything is under control. Cover it all up. If you do, you will feel guilt and more guilt. Spirals of pain and shame.

I learned to be kind because beneath every smile is a powerful story that can make you weep for years.

Social media has made people's lives seem bogus. Everyone thinks everyone's life is perfect except their own. However, everyone has his share of struggles; some are bigger than others and some are just the obstacles of daily life. Be kind, and know you are not alone.

Feeling Stuck

Many are sucked into the illusion of feeling stuck. You stay where you are in that dark closed cave, in an isolated place, not looking around you, thinking wrongly that you are disabled, paralyzed, and stuck. We are captives to our own limited abilities.

It's all an illusion. You are free. This mold that you are putting yourself in is a true lie. Look to the sides. There is no limit—except for the fact that you are looking down and are unable to notice your surroundings and have forgotten your capabilities. This cave is in front of you, and it's all you can see.

I am free—free of the captivity to which I once was bound with.

"The secret of happiness is freedom. The secret of freedom is courage." ~Thucydides

Exercise

We call ourselves names in our heads and sometimes even verbalize them. Society claims that it's unacceptable for us to abuse another human yet it's totally fine—and even normal—to abuse ourselves. We beat ourselves up saying things like, "I am fat, I am stupid, I am worthless, I am not enough, I am a weirdo." You can't tell someone else, "You are such a failure," so why is it ok to say it to yourself?! I have a confession: I used to be a bully. I am a recovering abuser—a self-abuser.

Make a promise to yourself to cease doing this to yourself, and when you catch yourself doing it, remind yourself that if it's not ok to say it to a friend, it's not ok to say it to yourself either. Be kind to yourself.

Why are we defensive sometimes with no reason? Because we attack ourselves in our own head. We misuse, abuse, and mistreat ourselves. I will choose for nothing to sink into my soul unless I hear it, filter it, and let in only what heals, what makes me grow, and what helps.

From now on I will work out and exercise emotionally and mentally, training myself to have extra strength and endurance for self appreciation rather than pride, for watching my negative thoughts rather than judging, but understanding and learning how to deal with it, to grow not to crawl—to grow wiser instead of falling on my knees unable to rise again and crawl like a baby. I will be fit and align my heart with my thoughts. No more fighting with who I am. I will make peace by performing emotional and mental exercises, widening my capacity to be more. They call it in psychology cognitive behavior.

It takes time to build muscles. It takes time to change bad habits. It takes time to grow, and it takes patience to see results. Join me and work out so we can see the blissful results together.

Mindfulness

The art of mindfulness: to maintain moment by moment awareness of ones own thoughts and feelings with our surroundings; to meditate instead of become overwhelmed; to repent and forgive rather than to guilt oneself or nest in the past; to make our best with what we have at the moment, to focus, pay attention, be awake with our hearts, be present in the present moment.

I know you will tell me it's not as easy as it sounds here. How can I practice the art of mindfulness if I go through a big loss such as a large amount of money or more significant—a dear loved one? It takes intentional effort to accept the situation, not to judge your emotions and thoughts, and to focus on your present moment. All of that can be achieved with training and meditation. Stop judging and start cooping with life. It's ok to smile and enjoy even if you have a great struggle.

Whenever a negative thought comes in, pause for a minute. Don't judge it. Just think. Try to understand its roots, and then try to calm the negativity of the thought—not by crushing it, but by understanding where it came from, naming the root and becoming aware. Then let go and try to enjoy your present moment.

"Therefore I tell you, do not worry about your life, what you will eat or drink; or about your body, what you will wear. Is not life more than food, and the body more than clothes? Look at the birds of the air; they do not sower reap or store away in barns, and yet your heavenly father feeds them. Are you not much more valuable than they? Can any of you by worrying add a single hour to your life?" Mathew 6:25-27

Transformation

Feeling crucified, inescapable pain, with tied fists? You might say, no one will ever feel me, for the heart only knows its own agony.

Humiliation, loneliness, great loss, old pain that has been engraved in your soul--You alone will feel the pain from these types of trials. No one can truly experience your pain with you, even if they say they do. They can only imagine.

However, with great pain, you will be liberated from some infatuations and hunger from earthly things. You will be freed from focusing on the imperfections of others and their deficiencies. Redirecting your pain will make you long for the perfection of God, the beauty of spiritual growth and the liberation that allows you to grow stronger and gain the beauty of patience. I could go on and on speaking about the wonders of patience, something that I missed having for a while and am humbly still working on acquiring. Is there a scientist that discovered a cure without countless trials and much patience? Is there a mother that had a baby in just three days without walking through the nine painful months prior to delivery with patience? Is there a geologist who investigated earth without hard work and patience? Is there a beautiful and strong butterfly that broke through its cocoon without patience? It may look like nothing is going on inside the cocoon, but big changes are happening. Not too soon and not too late: I will take my time to flourish.

Can this pain change to joy? Oh, yes! It can. The pain of sickness may turn into joy. The experience and the taste of pain can bring the joy of growth. The taste of agony, yes, can bring you joy. Be a beautiful butterfly, morph to joy, and your colors will shine and be vibrant.

A Dream

A dream of a year all spring, a soul with no sin, a body with no ache, and a world with nothing but love—let me dream.

For as long as I can remember, I wished for a year full of Spring. It refreshes me—those vibrant colors: green, red, blue, and orange. The perfect weather, not so cold yet not so hot: it's just right. Sunny and breezy. But then I thought if it was Spring all year round, I wouldn't have appreciated it that much.

Take this analogy for example. I love steak. (If you are vegetarian, substitute steak with beans. I love being compassionate and understanding our differences.) But if steak becomes my everyday meal, three times a day, I will get so used to it that I will stop appreciating it and will likely end up hating it.

Let's say here Spring equals hope, which is my dream. What if beyond getting a year of Spring I were given a perfect life—no ups or downs, neither hot nor cold, no mistakes, no pain: all just right. How would I ever grow? Without pain, I can't overcome. Without sorrow, I can't experience true joy. Without bitterness, I can't truly understand the concept of sweetness. Sunshine comes after rain, so does hope come after pain.

Hope comes after a lot of sweaty days full of hard work. My dream has changed as I have grown: I now long for Spring to come once in a while so I will be reminded and amazed by change and growth that takes place as a result of the other seasons.

Upside Down

Everything seems wrong. Oh, how crocked the world seems! It's just so evil!
What do you see? When I look at life, I see illness, evil, envy all around me. Wrong answer! Nope, life is not all bad. You can't have your head stuck in the ground and say, "All there is is dirt." Life has its fair share of unpleasant events, but it isn't all bad all the time.

There are some words that we often misuse: ALWAYS, EVERY TIME, EVERYTHING, ALL THE TIME, NEVER. Life is not ALWAYS horrible. There are some very beautiful days that we cherish. The world does not treat you badly EVERY TIME you try. EVERYTHING and EVERYONE is not ALWAYS against you. Still you have some friends even if they are very few. I will NEVER be able to do it, is not the right answer for success. He ALWAYS does that. She NEVER calls me. They NEVER hear me. Are these statements really ALWAYS true?

Lift your head from between your feet because if you stay down there too long, you will smell feet, and you won't enjoy the fresh air that you are provided. Try, smile, and see what's good. The glass is ALWAYS half full, I mean sometimes half full. Oops! I made that mistake too. I make it ALL the time. Haha! You got me again.

My Name

Hi. Let me introduce myself. My name is Regret.
I say things; then I beat myself to death. Why, oh why do I say the things I do, make the mistakes I do, and then feel shame and guilt after I do them?

What's your name? It may be Shame, it may be Defeat, it may be Dweller or Guilt, or Rage. Labels, labels, and more labels! You may not even be aware or conscious of the name assigned to you by yourself or others. Where did these names and labels come from? A parent, a teacher, a friend, a relative? Identify the root of these names that have been engraved in your soul, that you believed and started to act upon blindly whether they came from within or from the world. Whatever your name is, no matter how you are, your real name is Forgiven. Your name is Child of the Most High.

No matter what you have done, what you will do, or what you think you are, you are forgiven. Seek and you will find. Ask and it will be given. Be stuck no more. Live day by day and forgive yourself so you will be able to forgive others.

I am still trying to love. I am still learning to accept myself. And in the process, I am still learning to tear my old label and accept my new name: "Loved."

Volcano

When I get angry, triggered, or upset, my feelings become like a volcano. When pressure builds up, eruptions occur.

In an eruption, lava, poisonous gas, rocks will be thrown everywhere. It's just a pure mess. I am a mess, or is the world a mess? Perhaps both. I don't know. I leave myself with fire inside, and it explodes all over me leading to lots of ashes which suffocates myself and others. When I finally calm down, I am left with a disastrous atmosphere. I want to learn to control those feelings, those unleashed emotions.

All I know is that there is hope—hope for healing—but how can I heal from anger if there is injustice, hunger, illness, and a lot of anger? Where can hope be found here in this mess, in this myth that we are left in. I have contributed damage to the world through my imperfections, hurting others with my own hurt wondering who started it all first.

I have learned the different kinds of anger: the volcano anger that erupts and the silent, quiet rage anger, like a mosquito that bites you, carrying a deadly virus poisoning you and leaving you to die silently. Both kill; both are dangerous.

Now I've talked about anger and uncontrollable feelings, so where is the hope that I mentioned a while ago?

Hope is in learning; it is in forgiving others and forgiving yourself. Hope is in the Healer and the Maker. I said learning first. Learning what? Learning to "respond" to your triggers rather than to "react." What's the difference? To respond is to listen, breath, and express your feelings, concerns, or hurt in a humane manner, similar to first responder, a firefighter, who is trained to provide care. On the other hand, reacting is pushing back the same hurt with fierceness, leaving a mess behind similar to a reactor, a nuclear bomb, or a volcano. The reactor is transformed from a victim to an attacker. Learn to be in control of yourself; learn not to make everyone else the reason for your mistakes. And even if you make a mistake—a reaction—have hope in training yourself to be in control of yourself not others. Never give up on yourself claiming, "I am an angry person; that's just who I am." Hope in change for the better. Remember when we said don't label yourself and be stuck there with that label?

There is hope for me, hope for you, hope for those who have hope in change. Hope in having hope in others, hope for all.

Hope

Failure I feel. That whisper in my ear that I am worthless leaves me feeling as if there is no hope. Something inside of me keeps trying to convince me that I am mediocre at everything I do, that I am not good enough, that I am not smart enough. My voice gravels; my hands shake. I am so afraid to try. Something steals my joy, my confidence, and my trust whenever I try.

How will I be able to succeed if I stay afraid? How will I love life or love myself? How can anyone love when they are afraid? How will anyone love me if I am afraid to trust my abilities and myself?

Because I refuse to move, I feel despair—I feel wrecked. "But where will this take me?" my heart asks.

Here comes hope to pat me on my heart, to love me, telling me, "So what if you are not perfect? You are still loved." As a result of this reassurance—this hope—I break that sound of failure and block it from my mind. Through trials I will choose perseverance. I will smile; I will succeed. I am a loving, genuine person. You too! You are beautiful. Fill in the blanks and give yourself hope and love. Choose two strong characteristics about yourself and declare with conviction that you are those qualities: "I am a _____, _____ human worthy of love and grace.

Addiction

Sometimes it feels so right to do the wrong thing.
Addiction? Not just addiction to that thing or even that person; it consumes you to the point that it becomes you.

Some people, due to life's pain and what they have gone through, have deficiencies in their brain's reward system. These people never feel satisfied; they are never full. This leaves them trying to self medicate, which is more like hijacking the reward system in the brain. When it's difficult to taste pleasure as one used to, it's because of chronic inescapable stress. At the time one thinks it's helping him deal with emotional or physical pain he has gone through. It can lead to trauma, grief, depression, loss or pain. Our inability to deal with distressing emotions, pain from the past, or ongoing hurt leaves us craving something intensely, losing control as a result of misuse. Perhaps it's drugs, alcohol, gambling, smoking, pornography, shopping, or even over-working or engaging in an unhealthy relationship. Some are addicted to hating themselves. Some are addicted to thinking and worrying.

What if we chose to become addicted to things that make us better rather than worse? As for me, personally I have chosen to become addicted to peace, to joy, to loving people and loving myself. I am not a psychologist or a therapist here, but I can assure you that loving yourself is one of the most crucial steps to overcoming negative addictions.
I have dedicated myself to celebrating the gift of life. I will surrender to the Most High, to the Lover of mankind. No more numbness! You are so loved. Breath, celebrate, and enjoy life. Join me.

Free

Free the birds in the cage of your soul. Free those mistakes engraved on your heart that have taken their toll on you. I am freed; I am redeemed. I have no chains, no limits. I am the idea of light, reflected from the main source of light—from thee God of light—no longer bound to darkness. My heavy burdens are all gone. I can dance freely, knowing I am loved. No more dancing with evil in the devil's clutches.

Open the cage of my heart, Lord. Let all those past and imprisoning hurts fly away, be erased. Be released, be free, and fly freely.

Don't forget today before you sleep to claim freedom for your heart from any burdens. It will heal you; it will make you lighter, brighter, and in control. Forgive those who have hurt you. Then ask for forgiveness for yourself. Be free.

Surrender

I will let go of all my troubles, all my burdens. Those heavy chains keep me under ground, a dweller, crushed, and dormant thinking I am dead, knocked out, and disabled. I will leave it all behind and rise.

Follow your passion. Success comes when you follow your passion and your dream. I know it might sound cliché. It's not that I discovered gold here. But for long I thought, I can't do this, I can't do that because I didn't follow my passion. I was too afraid of people and of failure. But here I am writing this book, not trying to please, but just enjoying each word I write and each art piece I create. Like it? Awesome. Don't like? Fine by me. I will live because I will let go of my insecurity and enjoy who I am and what I am doing. I will fly far with my imagination and do what I like, hoping in my heart to inspire some to have perseverance and to surrender. I hope we choose to freeze all of those negative thoughts that sabotage us and imagine ourselves light and free and rising above our enemy who tries to pull us down. Choosing not to surrender is like having yourself chained to 2000 pounds wondering why you can't move, puzzled by your heaviness and disability. Break the chain and surrender. What are you scared of?

Know your call despite all those fears—no more sheltering oneself in the comfort zone. Everyday is a new day to strive and try. Through trails come strength. The choice to give up is bankruptcy from courage.

Surrendering is strength, is courage, is freedom.

Rise and Shine

I will rise—
Rise above emotional pain.
Rise above comparison and the need to compete.

Rise above stress, anxiety, and depression.
Rise above proving my point or disproving yours.
Rise above worrying about tomorrow.

Rise above putting others down to rise!
Rise above those who hurt me and kill them with kindness.
Rise above wanting to fit in.

Rise above perfection, but never give up affection.
Rise above judging myself if I fell down but I didn't rise.
I will rise again and again when I fall down.

Sure! You want to be successful and loved, but try to rise above the need of being accepted all the time.

Rise and shine, fellow humans, for the bottom is crowded, but the top is glorious!

Beauty from Ashes

From a dead end to deliverance, from ashes to beauty…

It seems that your life is all falling apart: everything is crashing, you are burned out, people make promises and break them, you fail at your job, your relationships are failing, everything is just breaking and burning. How can I deal with complete blaze and pain? Faith? Yeah, right! I am saying my life is falling apart, and you suggest faith? Where can I get this faith if I have none in anything now.

Faith is not pretending you don't have a problem. Faith is not saying, "I feel pretty good" even when life is falling apart. Faith is knowing that God will handle it, that He will deliver you. No denial—faith is not denying your struggles. It is knowing that everything will work for the best, and He will deliver you through this. When I start looking at the problem, I will completely sink. However, when I look beyond my circumstances, I will see the answer. Faith is not changing your trouble; it's changing how you look at it. It's redirecting your focus from the problem to the Solver.

What's the difference between gratitude and faith? Gratitude is thanking BECAUSE; faith is thanking EVEN THOUGH. What's the difference between healing and resurrecting? Healing is when you have a wound or pain and then it mends; resurrecting is when your life is dead, all gone, and then you are brought to life again. Which is stronger? You decide. Gratitude or Faith? Healing or Resurrecting? Because or even though?

The Perfect Place

Take me to the place where there are no countries. Where there are countries there are borders, there are wars, there are goodbyes. Take me to the place where there is no money. For where there is money, there are bills, there is greed, there is poverty. Take me to the place where there is no religion. Yes, I said religion. Where there is religion, there is hate, but take me to that place where there is relationship—true, authentic relationship—with God. Not just words, dos and don'ts, but pure love. Take me to the place where there are no friends, for where there are friends, there will be expectations, frustrations, and the potential for enemies. Rather take me to the place of one big family.

No, we don't want to die. We have a life of purpose to accomplish and fulfill. No matter how perfect our life may seem at times, there is no real perfection under the sun. Know that and live keeping your eyes on that place—the perfect place: Heaven.

"If I find in myself a desire which no experience in this world can satisfy, the most parable explanation is that I was made for anther world." C.S Lewis